basic flavorings

Mustard

Clare Gordon-Smith

photography by

James Merrell

COURAGE
BOOKS
AN IMPRINT OF RUNNING PRESS
PHILADELPHIA · LONDON

Art Director **Jacqui Small**

Art Editor **Penny Stock**

Designer **Megan Smith**

Editor **Elsa Petersen-Schepelern**

Photography **James Merrell**

Food Stylist **Clare Gordon-Smith**

Stylist **Sue Parker**

Production Manager **Kate Mackillop**

Printed and bound in Hong Kong

Library of Congress Cataloging-in-Publication number
96-66812

ISBN 0-7624-0200-8

This edition published in the United States of America in 1998 by
Courage Books, an imprint of
Running Press Book Publishers
125 South Twenty-second Street
Philadelphia, Pennsylvania 19103-4399

**My thanks to my family—my father,
sister and grandmother—to David
Hurcomb, Sarah Kidd, Annabel
Ford, Di Reeds, and James Merrell.**

Notes:
**Ovens should be preheated to the
specified temperature—if using a
convection oven, adjust time and
temperature according to the
manufacturer's instructions.**

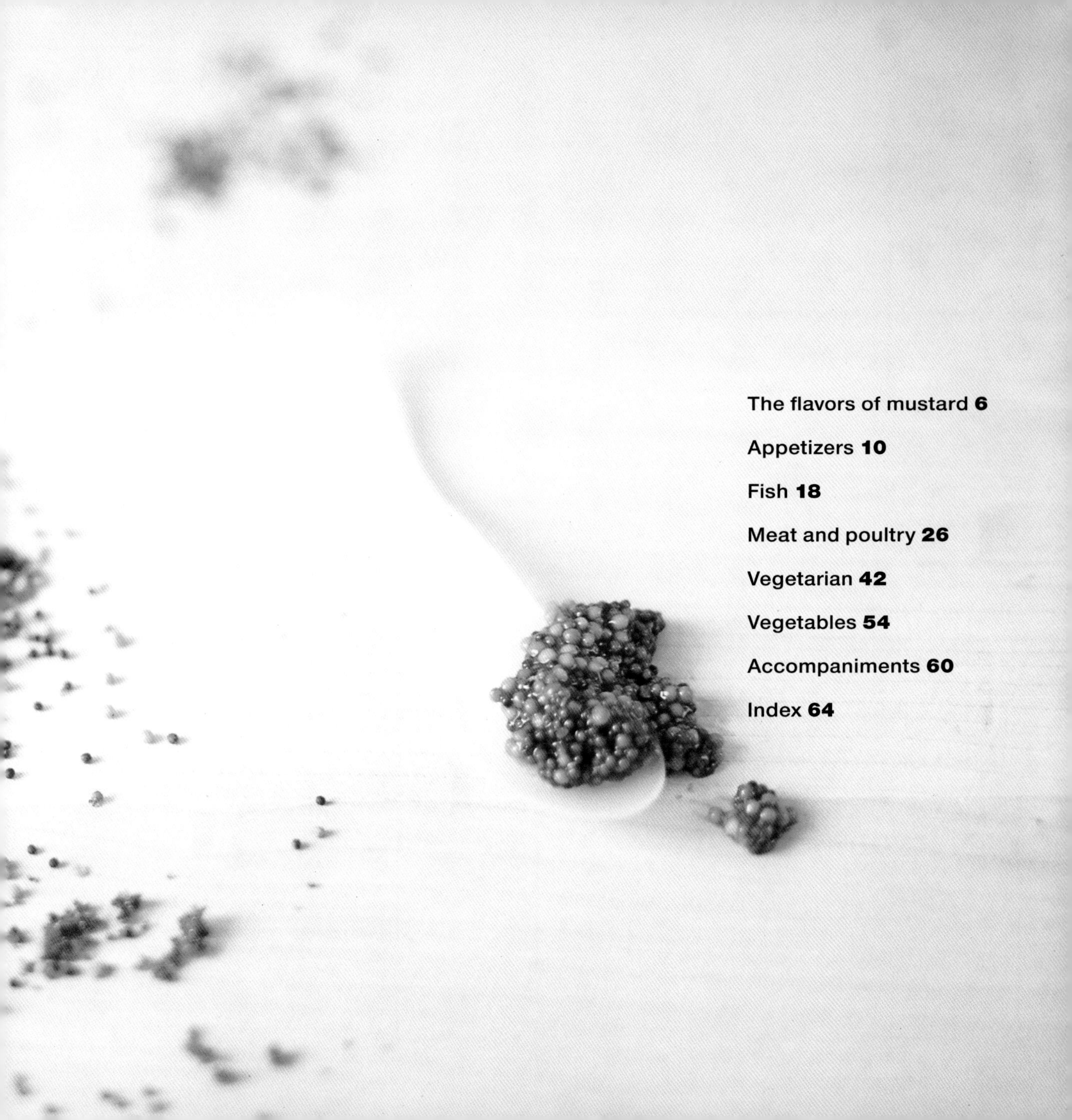

Mustard is best-known for its use as a condiment when mixed with wine, citrus juice, or vinegar. It varies in spiciness —from very hot English mustard (either powder or sauce), to mild French Dijon, and the mild sweet mustards of America, Scandinavia, and Germany, which often include sugar. However, the seeds of the mustard plant—spicy brown or black Indian mustard seeds, or milder European and American yellow mustard seeds—are the basis of many marvelous spicy mixes. **Mustard butter** (rear left) is wonderful on bread or dotted on broiled meats. Yellow mustard seeds, mixed with cinnamon and cloves, make a traditional **pickling mix** (front left). A **curry powder** mixture (front centre) is a European version of the complex and varied *masala* mixtures of true Indian cuisine. It includes turmeric, coriander seeds, dried chiles, pepper, cumin, and black Indian mustard seeds. Mustard is also part of many French vinaigrette dressings, including this **mustard vinaigrette** (front right), mixed with olive oil, wine vinegar, salt, and pepper. It can be made with crunchy wholegrain mustard (as here), or with mild French Dijon or hot English mustard powder (right rear) for slightly different tastes.

the flavors of

Mustard

wholegrain mustard

chile mustard

hot English mustard

yellow mustard powder

Finely ground mustard seeds are the basis of mustard powder, which is then blended with wine, beer, citrus juices, or vinegar to form creamy sauces like bright yellow hot **English mustard**, **cider mustard**, soft yellow **Dijon mustard**, and other mixes, usually including whole seeds, **8** The flavors of mustard

such as **wholegrain mustard** and **moutarde à l'ancienne**. Other flavorings, such as fresh or dried chiles can also be added to produce **chile mustard**, with heat depending on the spiciness of both the mustard and the chiles. **Chinese mustard** is the hottest of all. Other mustard products include **mustard oil**,

moutarde à l'ancienne

yellow mustard seeds

Dijon mustard

black mustard seeds

which releases marvelous aromas when heated, and is widely used in India and Nepal as a massage oil. **Mustard greens**, large and small, are often part of the salad mixes sold in supermarkets—the larger the leaves, the spicier they are (see page 38). They are also used as a side dish in American Soul Food cooking and are available fresh or canned. Chinese preserved mustard greens, with a sweet-and-sour taste, are used as a vegetable or flavoring ingredient in soups or stir-fries. Pretty **mustard cress** are the sprouted seeds of mustard and cress. Sold in punnets in supermarkets, they are easy to sprout yourself.

Appetizers

Mussel soup
with mustard and cream

Mustard powder is usually made into a sauce with an acidic ingredient such as vinegar, wine, cider, or citrus juice to point up the flavors. Mustards bought ready-made can be kept for up to a year before they start to lose their strength. Adding the mustard at the end of this recipe helps retain its spicy flavor.

Place the cleaned mussels in a large pan with the onion and herbs. Add the wine or cider, season with cayenne pepper, cover with a lid, and simmer for 5 to 10 minutes, until the mussels open (discard any that remain closed). Remove the pan from the heat and transfer the mussels to heated serving bowls. Mix the mustard with the cream, stir into the pan juices, taste, and adjust the seasoning (take care, as mussels are often naturally quite salty). Pour the liquid over the mussels, sprinkle them with the extra thyme leaves, and serve.

4 lb. cleaned mussels, in the shell*

1 onion, finely chopped

1 tablespoon finely chopped parsley

1 teaspoon chopped fresh thyme leaves, plus extra, to serve

½ bay leaf

1¾ cups white wine or cider

a pinch of cayenne pepper

2 teaspoons hot, ready-made English mustard

½ cup heavy cream

sea salt and freshly ground black pepper (optional)

Serves 4

*Farmed mussels usually have clean shells. If not, scrub them with a stiff brush and pull off the beards. Tap the shells against a hard surface and discard any that don't open.

Swedish pea soup
with Dijon mustard

¾ cup yellow split peas

4 cups hot ham stock

2 onions, halved lengthwise

1 carrot, thickly sliced

3 fresh bay leaves

4 tablespoons Dijon mustard

salt and freshly ground black pepper

to serve

4 tablespoons crème fraîche

snipped chives or parsley

Serves 4

This recipe, an update on a traditional Scandinavian dish, was shown to me by a Danish friend, and I tasted a soup very like it on my recent visit to Sweden. Scandinavia is an interesting region, with delicious, modern cuisines full of bright, clear tastes as well as wonderful, warming winter dishes like this.

Place the first 5 ingredients in a large saucepan and bring to a boil. Reduce the heat and simmer for about 20 minutes. Test the peas—they should be whole, but soft. If not, cook for 5 to 10 minutes more (the time will depend on the age of the peas). Remove the bay leaves and either serve the soup as it is or, for a smoother texture, purée in a blender or food processor, in batches if necessary. Stir in the mustard and seasoning.
Serve the soup topped with a tablespoon of crème fraîche and snipped chives or parsley.

a modern update on a traditional

mustard-flavored dish from **Scandinavia**

Smoked mackerel pâté

A quick, easy, and utterly delicious pâté served with toast and spicy mustard butter. The butter can be used in other ways—try it melted over broiled steak or steamed corn.

Purée the mackerel fillets in a blender with the light cream and crème fraîche. Spoon into small dishes or ramekins and chill in the refrigerator. Cream the mustard with a little water, then stir into the butter and serve in little cups, together with the dishes of pâté and a stack of toast.

1 lb. fillets of smoked mackerel, skinned

⅔ cup light cream

⅔ cup crème fraîche

toast, to serve

mustard butter

2 teaspoons prepared English mustard

6 tablespoons sweet butter, softened

Serves 4

Parma ham salad
with mustard leaves and dressing

Mustard leaf is widely used in the salad mixes sold by supermarkets. It has a zippy peppery taste, reinforced here with crunchy mustard seeds in the dressing. Papaya can be substituted instead of the melon.

Halve and seed the melon, then cut the flesh into pieces with a knife, teaspoon, or melon baller. Place the salad leaves on a serving plate. Roll the Parma ham into cigar-shapes and add to the salad, together with the pieces of melon and the tomatoes, cut in half. Mix all the dressing ingredients together, pour over the salad, then serve.

1 honeydew melon

mixed salad leaves, such as mustard leaves and mustard cress

8 slices Parma ham

8 oz. cherry tomatoes

French dressing

2 tablespoons wholegrain mustard

4 tablespoons olive oil

1 teaspoon lemon juice

2 teaspoons honey

Serves 4

German potato salad
with mustard caper mayonnaise

This hearty German-style salad is pure
comfort food—wonderfully creamy, but with
the verve, crunch, and bite of wholegrain
mustard and capers in the dressing. For
a true northern-European flavor, add some
finely chopped fresh dill to the dressing.

Place the potatoes in a pan of cold salted water,
bring to a boil, and simmer for about 20 minutes,
or until tender.
Mix the dressing ingredients together and set aside
to develop the flavors.
Chop the frankfurters into 1-inch sections.
Separate the endive leaves and arrange on a plate.
Drain the warm potatoes and mix into the dressing,
stir in the frankfurters, then spoon onto the serving
plate, on top of the endive leaves.
Sprinkle with parsley and serve.

an easy recipe, with crunchy

mustard mayonnaise and capers

1 lb. waxy yellow salad
potatoes, such as
Yukon Gold

8 oz. cooked
frankfurters

3 heads Belgian endive

about 6 tablespoons
chopped fresh
flat-leaf parsley

**mustard caper
mayonnaise**

⅔ cup sour cream

1 tablespoon
wholegrain mustard

⅔ cup mayonnaise

2 teaspoons capers

sea salt and freshly
ground black pepper

Serves 4

Fish

Roasted salmon fillet
with leeks and mustard

Salmon is a very rich fish, with a flavor that is much-enhanced by the crunchy, spicy bite of wholegrain mustard. Heating mustard releases its volatile oils so all the aroma and flavor can be appreciated.

Mix the mustard into the crème fraîche, then stir in the sliced leeks. Spread the mixture over the base of an ovenproof roasting pan, place the salmon fillets on top, and cook in a preheated oven at 400°F for 10 to 15 minutes until tender, but pink in the middle. Serve the salmon with the leek and mustard sauce, sprinkled with snipped chives, and accompanied by new potatoes and char-grilled asparagus.

2 teaspoons wholegrain mustard

4 tablespoons crème fraîche

2 small leeks, trimmed and sliced

4 salmon fillets

a bunch of fresh chives, snipped

to serve

boiled new potatoes

char-grilled asparagus spears

Serves 4

Little fish pies
with hot mustard sauce

English mustard powder is usually sold in cans to exclude both air and light—one of the best ways of keeping mustard fresh. Try to buy mustard powder little and often, because it gradually loses much of its punch. Mustard powder should always be mixed with cold liquids, not hot, or the mixture will be very bitter. Mustard isn't traditional in a fish pie, but I think it livens up the flavor very well.

6 tablespoons sweet butter

8 oz. cod, cubed

8 oz. fresh salmon, cubed

8 oz. peeled uncooked shrimp

3 tablespoons all-purpose flour

1½ cups fish stock

½ cup heavy cream

3 tablespoons chopped fresh flat-leaf parsley

1½ tablespoons chopped fresh tarragon

2 teaspoons hot English mustard

8 oz. short-crust pastry

salt and freshly ground black pepper

Serves 4

Melt the butter in a large skillet, add the fish and shrimp, and cook until the fish turns milky-white. Remove the fish and shrimp with a slotted spoon, put on a plate, and set aside to keep warm. Stir the flour into the butter, and cook gently, stirring, for about 1 to 2 minutes to allow the starch grains to burst. Gradually stir in the fish stock and cook gently until thickened. Mix the heavy cream, herbs, and mustard together in a bowl, then stir into the skillet. Taste and adjust the seasoning, then gently fold in the fish. Divide the mixture between 4 small pie dishes, about 1 cup each.
Roll out the short-crust pastry and cut 4 circles a little larger than the top of the dishes. Put the pastry on top of the pies and trim the edges by cutting at right angles with a knife. Cook in a preheated oven at 400°F for 20 minutes until the top is crisp and golden. Serve with new potatoes and a green vegetable.

Pan-fried halibut
with mustard seed tomato sauce

Yellow European mustard seeds are slightly less pungent than the black Indian variety, and give this sauce extra texture as well as flavor. If halibut is unavailable, use any other firm-fleshed white fish, such as cod—though salmon could also be used.

4 halibut steaks, about 8 oz. each

¼ cup unsalted butter

1 tablespoon olive oil

tomato sauce

1 teaspoon olive oil

2 shallots, chopped

1 lb. plum tomatoes, peeled and chopped

1 garlic clove, crushed

1 teaspoon yellow mustard seeds, crushed

1 pinch sugar

to serve

lemon wedges

sprigs of parsley

Serves 4

To make the tomato sauce, heat the olive oil in a skillet, add the shallots, and sauté until soft and translucent. Add the tomatoes, garlic, mustard seeds, and sugar and cook until the tomatoes soften. Heat the butter and olive oil in a separate skillet, add the fish, and pan-fry until golden on each side. Serve the fish with lemon wedges, parsley sprigs, and the tomato sauce on the side.

an easy, zippy recipe with

crunch and spicy flavor

Roasted cod
with mustard mash

I have used a large piece of cod, the middle
cut, known as the saddle. You may have
to ask your fish seller to cut it specially.
The result is very stylish for an important
dinner party. I first encountered this dish
in Göteburg, Sweden, cooked by Chef Leif
Manneström at the Sjömagazinet—a glorious
fish restaurant overlooking the water, with
blue-checked tablecloths and blue pots of
equally blue pansies. Northern Europe has
a huge repertoire of great potato recipes
such as this mustard-flavored mash.

Mix all the hazelnut topping ingredients together in a
bowl. Put the fish in a roasting pan and press the
breadcrumbs over the top.
Cook in a preheated oven at 400°F for 25 to
35 minutes or until the fish turns milky-white.
Cook the potatoes a pan of boiling salted water until
soft and tender. Drain and mash well, stir in the
mustard and butter, then beat in enough milk to
produce the consistency you prefer.
Serve the cod with the mustard mash and
a sprig of parsley.

2 lb. saddle of cod

sprigs of parsley,
to serve

hazelnut topping

½ cup breadcrumbs

½ cup flat-leaf parsley,
chopped, plus sprigs,
to serve

⅓ cup hazelnuts,
crushed

salt and freshly ground
black pepper

mustard mash

2 lb. floury potatoes

2 teaspoons
English mustard,
mixed to a paste with
1 tablespoon water

4 tablespoons
sweet butter

hot milk (see method)

Serves 4

Meat and poultry

Roasted chicken
with honey-mustard crust

This honey-mustard glaze gives a delicious
spicy-sweet crunchy crust. If you don't have
wholegrain mustard, use mustard powder or
Dijon. For a quick supper, substitute chicken
pieces or coarse-textured pork sausages.

Put the mustard, honey, soy sauce, and orange rind
and juice in a bowl and mix well.
Put the chicken in a roasting pan and spread the
honey and mustard mixture over the breast.
Cook in a preheated oven at 350°F for about 1 hour,
or until tender and the juice runs clear when the
chicken is pierced with a skewer through the thickest
part of the thigh.
Remove the chicken from the pan and set aside to
keep warm. Pour off all except 1 tablespoon of the
juices and transfer the pan to the top of the stove.
Raise the heat to high, stir in the flour, and cook,
stirring, for about 1 minute to burst the starch grains.
Pour the chicken stock into the pan and cook,
stirring, until the gravy is well-thickened. Serve the
chicken with vegetables and a pitcher of gravy.

2 tablespoons
wholegrain mustard

3 tablespoons honey

1 drop soy sauce

grated rind and juice
of 1 orange

1 chicken, about 3 lb.

1 tablespoon
all-purpose flour

1¼ cups chicken stock

Serves 4

Chicken phyllo pie
with mustard and leeks

The flavors of mustard and leeks seem to have an affinity for each other, judging from the number of classic dishes based on these ingredients. This comforting family dish is quickly made with cooked chicken, available from most supermarkets (or you can cook extra next time you serve roasted chicken).

Melt the butter, stir in the leeks, and let soften. Stir in the flour, cook for 1 minute, then stir in the milk and mustard. Bring to a boil, then reduce the heat and simmer for about 3 minutes. Let cool, then stir in the cold chicken. To prepare the pastry, melt the butter and brush one side of 6 of the sheets of pastry with the butter. Insert, in layers, in a 8- to 9-inch pie dish. Overlap the excess around the edges. Spoon the chicken mixture into the dish, then arrange any excess pastry over the top of the chicken. Fold the remaining 2 sheets of phyllo into rolls, cut into strips about 1 inch wide, then loosely tie the strips into knots. Arrange the pastry knots on top of the pie and brush with melted butter. Cook in a preheated oven at 350°F for 40 to 50 minutes or until the pastry is golden brown.

2 tablespoons sweet butter

2 leeks, trimmed and sliced

2½ tablespoons all-purpose flour

1¼ cups milk

2 tablespoons herb mustard or American mustard

1 lb. cooked chicken, cut into large chunks

8 sheets phyllo pastry

¼ cup sweet butter

Serves 4

Pork frikadeller
meatballs with tomato sauce

Meatballs—known as *frikadeller* in Danish—
are a favorite dish all over Scandinavia,
and often flavored with mustard (another
popular Scandinavian ingredient). Pork is
widely used in the region, as is veal, and
these meatballs are often made with a
ground mixture of these two meats.

Put the breadcrumbs in a bowl, add milk, soak for
10 minutes, then squeeze dry.
Mix in the ground pork, herbs, mustard, and
seasonings. Dampen your hands with water, then use
them to roll the mixture into walnut-sized balls.
Heat the oil in a wide skillet and sauté the meatballs
over a medium heat until nicely browned. Remove
with a slotted spoon, drain on paper towels, then
transfer to an ovenproof serving dish.
To make the tomato sauce, heat the olive oil in a
skillet, add the onion and garlic, then sauté gently
until softened and translucent. Stir in the remaining
ingredients. Pour the sauce over the meatballs and
bake in a preheated oven at 400°F for about
30 minutes until sizzling and bubbling.

a **mildly spicy** dish from Scandinavia

—made with **hot yellow mustard**

3 tablespoons
dry breadcrumbs

½ cup whole milk

12 oz. ground pork

2 tablespoons chopped
fresh flat-leaf parsley

2 teaspoons mixed
English mustard

vegetable oil,
for cooking

sea salt and freshly
ground black pepper

tomato sauce

2 tablespoons olive oil

1 onion, chopped

2 garlic cloves,
chopped

1 lb. chopped tomatoes

1 tablespoon
tomato purée

1–2 teaspoons sugar

salt and freshly
ground black pepper

Serves 4

Cabbage rolls
with steamed coconut rice

A European dish with an Asian twist. This time, the spicy heat is provided by yellow mustard powder instead of chiles. The influence is from Thailand, which has long-established trading links with Europe.

Blanch the cabbage leaves in boiling salted water for 1 minute, then drain.
Heat a skillet oven a gentle heat, then add the pork and sauté it in its own juices until browned. Stir in the mustard powder, scallions, and soy sauce.
Put 1 tablespoon of the mixture into the center of each cabbage leaf and roll up. Place in a roasting pan, pour in the chicken stock, and cover with foil.
Cook in a preheated oven at 400°F for 30 minutes.
Meanwhile, to make the coconut rice, put the rice in a pan with the coconut milk and water, bring to a boil uncovered, then cover with a lid, reduce the heat, and simmer for about 12 minutes or until done.
All the liquid should have been absorbed by the rice, but if not, drain through a strainer.
Serve with the cabbage rolls.

8 leaves from a Savoy cabbage, trimmed

1 lb. ground pork

1 teaspoon English mustard powder

1 bunch scallions, chopped

1 teaspoon dark soy sauce

1¼ cups chicken stock

steamed coconut rice

1 cup Thai jasmine rice

1 cup coconut milk

1 cup water

Serves 4

a succulent, spicy dish with

Asian and European influences

Broiled spareribs
with mustard and lime

Mustard mixed with a liquid, especially an acidic one like vinegar, wine, or citrus juice, develops its full heat and complexity of taste. It's wonderful here mixed with lime juice in a glaze for spareribs which are then broiled, char-grilled, or barbecued.

1 lb. pork spareribs

mustard glaze

6 tablespoons tomato ketchup

4 tablespoons English mustard

3–4 drops Worcestershire sauce

grated rind and juice of 2 limes

to serve

baked potatoes

mixed salad leaves with mustard vinaigrette (see pages 15, 56)

lime wedges

Serves 4

Mix the mustard glaze ingredients together in a small bowl. Put the spareribs in a flat roasting pan, then spread with the glaze. If time allows, cover and chill for 30 minutes to 1 hour to develop the flavors. When ready to cook, roast in a preheated oven at 400°F for 40 minutes.
Serve with baked potatoes, lime wedges, and mixed salad leaves tossed in a mustard vinaigrette.

try this **rhubarb confit** as an interesting

change from the more familiar **applesauce**

Loin of pork
with poached rhubarb confit

Since pork and apples are a traditional combination, in this recipe I have used cider mustard, made with apple cider. If you can't find it, use any reasonably mild mustard, such as Dijon, American, or French.

Mash the mustard, orange zest, chopped parsley, and crushed garlic into a paste.
Make small cuts in the fat of the pork loin and push the paste into the cuts. Season with salt and pepper. Put the pork in a roasting pan, pour over the wine, then cook in a preheated oven at 375°F for 1 hour. Turn the meat over, season with salt and pepper, then roast for a further 30 minutes.
To make the confit, put the sugar in the pan with 2¾ cups cold water. Stir over a low heat until the sugar has dissolved, then bring to a boil. Simmer for 5 minutes. Trim the rhubarb and cut into 2-inch lengths. Drop into the sugar syrup, bring back to a simmer, and poach gently for 2 to 3 minutes until just tender but not collapsing. Drain and keep warm.
Lift the meat onto a warmed serving dish and arrange the rhubarb around it. Serve the remaining juices separately in a small pitcher.

2 tablespoons smooth cider mustard

a strip of orange zest

2 tablespoons chopped fresh flat-leaf parsley

2 garlic cloves, crushed

3½ lb. loin of pork, chined and skinned

2 cups dry white wine

sea salt and freshly ground black pepper

rhubarb confit

1¼ cups sugar

1 lb. fresh rhubarb

Serves 4

Steak sandwich
with tomatoes and mustard leaves

Mustard is a traditional accompaniment to a steak sandwich. Barbecue or char-grill the steak at a high temperature, then serve in a split ciabatta loaf spread with a little butter. The mustard leaves used here are delicious, but if they are difficult to find, use plain lettuce, or peppery watercress instead. Because this dish calls for a lot of mustard, I suggest you use the milder Dijon-style.

2 tablespoons sweet butter

1 tablespoon Dijon mustard, plus extra, to serve

2 rump steaks, about 1 lb. each

1 ciabatta bread, split

sweet butter, for spreading

salad leaves, such as mustard leaves

sliced ripe red plum tomatoes

salt and freshly ground black pepper

Serves 4

Cream the butter with the mustard, dot a little on each steak, heat the broiler or stove-top grill pan, and cook the steaks for a few minutes on each side. Spread a little butter in the ciabatta bread, add the salad leaves and tomatoes, top with the steaks, and season to taste. Cut the loaf crosswise into 4 servings and serve extra mustard separately.

full-grown **mustard leaves** are hot and peppery—**baby leaves** are milder, but still spicy

Beef carbonade

Beef carbonade is the classic Belgian beef-
and-beer dish, in this case topped with slices
of French baguette, spread with mustard.

Melt the butter or oil in a large skillet. Add the meat
and cook over a high heat, stirring until well
browned. Remove and set aside. Sauté the bacon in
the skillet until crisp. Add the onions and cook over a
low heat until soft and translucent. Add the
mushrooms and cook for 2 minutes, then stir in the
flour. Transfer the bacon, onions, and mushrooms to
a large casserole dish, season with salt and pepper,
then add the sugar, mace, and allspice.
Mix well and pour over the Guinness. Add enough
water just to cover the ingredients, then add the bay
leaves and cover tightly.
Bring to a boil on top of the stove, then transfer to a
preheated oven and cook at 325°F for 2 hours until
the meat is very tender. Remove the bay leaves, add
the parsley, then taste and adjust the seasoning.
To make the topping, spread the sliced baguette with
mustard, then arrange the slices in a circle around
the edge of the casserole. Return to the oven and
cook for a further 30 minutes.
Serve with mashed potatoes and green vegetables.

2 tablespoons
vegetable oil or butter

2 lb. stewing beef,
cut into 1-inch cubes

3 slices bacon,
chopped

2 large onions, chopped

4 oz. firm button
mushrooms,
thickly sliced

2½ tablespoons flour

2 tablespoons
soft brown sugar

1 pinch ground mace

1 pinch ground allspice

1¼ cups Guinness
or other stout,
or dark beer

2 bay leaves

3 tablespoons finely
chopped fresh parsley

1 French baguette
loaf, sliced

2 tablespoons
wholegrain mustard

salt and freshly
ground black pepper

Serves 4

Vegetarian

Leek and mustard tart

The filling for this modern update on the traditional quiche is full of sweet and mild ingredients—leeks, cream, and cheese—so the zip and crunch of wholegrain mustard adds some welcome spice.

Roll out the pastry and use to line 6 small tart pans, 8 inches in diameter, or 1 large one. Chill for 10 minutes, then fill with foil and dried beans or ceramic baking beans. Bake blind in a preheated oven at 400°F for 15 minutes. Remove from the oven and remove the foil and beans. Leave the oven on. Meanwhile, melt the butter in a skillet and gently sauté the leeks for 10 minutes until tender, adding a couple of tablespoons of water if necessary. Beat the eggs in a bowl, then stir in the crème fraîche, mustard, leeks, cheese, chives, and seasoning. Pour the mixture into the pastry case or cases and bake at 400°F for about 20 minutes until golden brown.
Serve warm or cold with a green salad.

8 oz. short-crust pastry

2 tablespoons unsalted butter

1 lb. leeks, trimmed and sliced

2 eggs

⅔ cup crème fraîche

2–3 tablespoons wholegrain mustard

4 oz. goat cheese

1 tablespoon snipped chives

sea salt and freshly ground black pepper

Serves 4

Indian vegetable curry

Mustard seeds, like many other spices, release their finest flavors when exposed to heat, and a common cooking method in India is to sauté the seeds until they pop (put a lid on the pan, or they'll bounce all over the place). India, with its enormous vegetarian population, is the source of many of the most exciting ways to cook vegetables.

If using desiccated coconut, soak in cold water for 10 minutes. Drain and squeeze dry in a clean cloth. Put the eggplants, peas, beans, and potato in a saucepan of boiling water and cook for about 5 minutes until just tender.

Heat the oil in a skillet, add the chiles, mustard seeds, salt, and garam masala, and sauté gently for a few minutes until the seeds begin to pop. Add the tomatoes and ½ cup water. Stir and simmer gently for a few minutes, stir in the drained vegetables and yogurt, and simmer for a further 10 minutes. Transfer to a serving dish and garnish with fresh cilantro and cashews.

½ cup freshly grated coconut, or ⅛ cup desiccated coconut

2 eggplants, diced

1¼ cups fresh peas

8 oz. green beans, cut into 1-inch pieces

1 potato, cut into fine matchsticks

1 tablespoon corn oil

2 green chiles, seeded and sliced

2 teaspoons black mustard seeds

1¼ teaspoons salt

1 teaspoon garam masala*

6 chopped tomatoes

3 tablespoons plain yogurt

chopped fresh cilantro

2 tablespoons toasted cashews

Serves 4

*From Asian food shops or spice counters, or use a pinch each of ground cinnamon and cloves.

Ratatouille gratin
with crunchy mustard topping

Ratatouille is the famous vegetable stew from Provence, made with wonderful, ripe, colorful ingredients like eggplants, bell peppers, tomatoes, and zucchinis. This version is topped with crunchy Parmesan and breadcrumbs, spiced with Dijon mustard—easily the most famous of all French mustards. Serve this gratin with a highly flavored main course, or as a vegetarian dish with a crisp green salad.

Heat the olive oil in a skillet, add the onion and garlic, and gently sauté until softened and translucent. Add the remaining vegetables and gently sauté for 20 minutes. Add the thyme, tomato paste, salt, pepper, and 2 tablespoons water to the mixture, then spoon into a ovenproof dish.
Mix the topping ingredients together, sprinkle over the vegetables, then cook in a preheated oven at 350°F for 30 to 40 minutes until browned, then serve with a salad.

3 tablespoons olive oil

1 red onion, sliced

2 garlic cloves, crushed

1 small eggplant, sliced and diced

1 yellow bell pepper, seeded and diced

1 red bell pepper, seeded and diced

4 ripe tomatoes, coarsely chopped

2 yellow zucchinis thickly sliced

1 cauliflower separated into florets

1 teaspoon fresh thyme leaves

2 tablespoons tomato paste

salt and pepper

mustard topping

4 tablespoons fresh breadcrumbs

2 tablespoons grated Parmesan cheese

2 teaspoons smooth Dijon mustard

Serves 4

Spanakopita
Greek spinach and ricotta pies

A modern update on *spanakopita*, one of Greece's best-known dishes, and deservedly so. It is wonderful as a first course served with salad, as a light main course for lunch, or as finger food at parties. It usually includes eggs and onions, but these have been omitted for a lighter result. Mustard is not a traditional ingredient for these crunchy pies, but I find it adds welcome spice to the filling. Dijon is a milder form of mustard and won't overwhelm the mild and salty cheeses.

To make the filling, heat the oil in a pan, add the garlic, and sauté for about 1 minute until golden. Add the spinach and sauté until the spinach begins to wilt (about 1 minute). Remove from the heat and let cool. Mix the cheeses together in a bowl with the mustard, lemon juice, and lemon zest. Brush the phyllo pastry sheets with the melted butter, then layer 4 sheets in an 8- x 10-inch jelly roll pan. Add a layer of the spinach, then a layer of the ricotta cheese filling. Brush the remaining 4 sheets of pastry with butter and place on top. Cook in a preheated oven at 350°F for 25 minutes. Remove from the oven, let cool for 5 minutes, then cut into squares and serve warm or cold with salad leaves and crusty bread.

8 sheets phyllo pastry

6 tablespoons sweet
butter, melted

**spinach and
ricotta filling**

1 tablespoon olive oil

1 garlic clove, crushed

12 oz. baby spinach

½ cup ricotta cheese

½ cup feta cheese

2 teaspoons
Dijon mustard

1 tablespoon
lemon juice

1 teaspoon
grated lemon zest

Serves 4

Sweet potato gratin

The sharp, spicy taste of mustard points up
the sweetness of leeks and sweet potatoes in
this vegetarian side dish that non-vegetarians
will also enjoy. I cook this gratin with crunchy
wholegrain mustard because I like its
texture, but you could substitute other
mustards, such as Dijon, cider, or English.

2 lb. sweet potatoes,
sliced

1 lb. leeks, sliced

1¼ cups crème fraîche

½ cup whole milk

2 teaspoons
wholegrain mustard

2 tablespoons
sweet butter

½ cup grated
Cheddar cheese

sea salt and freshly
ground black pepper

Serves 4

Cook the sweet potatoes in boiling salted water for
about 5 minutes, then drain.
Steam the leeks for a few minutes (they can be
cooked in a steamer over the boiling sweet potatoes).
Transfer the sweet potatoes and leeks to an
ovenproof dish. Mix the crème fraîche, milk, and
mustard together, then spoon over the vegetables.
Dot the butter over the top, sprinkle with the grated
cheese, salt, and freshly ground black pepper, then
cook in a preheated oven at 350°F for 30 to
40 minutes. Serve with other vegetarian dishes.

Hot mustard pumpkin
in buckwheat pancakes

Buckwheat is a flavorful, highly nutritious ingredient for vegetarian cooking—and the mustard powder used in this crêpe mix makes it taste even more interesting. The sweetness of pumpkin and the crunchy spice of the mustard produce a delicious and interesting filling.

To make the pancakes, put the first 7 ingredients in a food processor and blend until smooth. Alternatively, put the flour and mustard powder in a bowl, lightly beat in the eggs, then add the milk, salt, and butter and beat until smooth. Melt the butter in a crêpe pan, then add 1 tablespoon of batter and swirl the pan around to coat the base. Let cook until small bubbles appear on the surface. Remove the pancake to a plate and keep it warm. Repeat until all the mixture is used. To make the filling, heat the oil in a skillet, add the onion, and cook until softened and translucent. Add the tomatoes and pumpkin, sauté gently until cooked, then stir in the mustard and pignoli nuts. Put a small amount of filling in each pancake, fold up, place in a heatproof serving dish, and sprinkle with the cheese. Cook under a preheated broiler for about 2 minutes until golden and bubbling, then serve sprinkled with chopped flat-leaf parsley.

⅓ cup buckwheat flour

⅓ cup all-purpose flour

2 eggs

1¼ cups whole milk

1 pinch salt

3 tablespoons sweet butter, melted

1 teaspoon mustard powder

1 tablespoon butter, for frying

chopped flat-leaf parsley, to serve

hot mustard pumpkin filling

2 tablespoons olive oil

1 onion, sliced

1 lb. tomatoes, sliced

1 butternut pumpkin, peeled and cut into small dice

2 teaspoons Dijon or American mustard

⅓ cup pignoli nuts, toasted

1 cup grated cheese

Serves 4

Vegetables

Hot beets
with herb mustard sauce

This dish can be served as an appetizer with rye bread—or as an accompaniment to strong-tasting meats like beef, pâté, or game. I have chosen baby beets, but you could also use larger ones.

Cook the beets in a pan of boiling salted water for about 20 to 30 minutes.
To make the sauce, melt the butter in a saucepan, stir in the flour, cook for 1 minute, then gradually stir in the milk, bring to a boil, and simmer for a few minutes until thickened. Stir in the mustard.
Drain the cooked beets, slip off the skins, (cut the beets into wedges if large), then place on a serving platter, and pour over the sauce.
Serve warm, sprinkled with chives.

2 lb. baby beets, soaked in cold water for 10 minutes, then rinsed carefully without breaking the skin

mustard sauce

2 tablespoons sweet butter

2 tablespoons all-purpose flour

1 cup whole milk

2 teaspoons Dijon or herb mustard

2 tablespoons chopped fresh chives

Serves 4

Spicy eggplants

Indian cooks have spice boxes containing small quantities of their favourite aromatics. Used in many different combinations, the spices give Indian dishes their wonderful, distinctive flavors. Black (actually very dark brown) mustard seeds are very often used, as in this simple vegetable curry.

Dip the tomatoes in boiling water for 1 minute, slip off the skins, cut in quarters, and seed. Heat the oil in a skillet, add the mustard and coriander seeds, onion, garlic, and chiles, and sauté gently. Stir in the eggplants, tomatoes, and seasonings, and cook gently for 10 to 15 minutes. Serve garnished with fresh cilantro.

1 lb. tomatoes

2 tablespoons corn oil

1 teaspoon black mustard seeds

1 teaspoon crushed coriander seeds

1 onion, chopped

1 garlic clove, crushed

2 green chiles, seeded and chopped

2 eggplants, sliced

salt and pepper

fresh cilantro, to serve

Serves 4

Simple potato salad

Toss the potatoes in the dressing while they are still warm so they will take up all the flavors of the Dijon vinaigrette.

Cook the potatoes in boiling salted water, for about 20 minutes or until just tender, then drain well. Mix all the dressing ingredients together in a salad bowl, then add the potatoes and mix gently until well covered with the dressing.

1 lb. new potatoes

Dijon dressing

2 teaspoons Dijon mustard

1 teaspoon honey

3 tablespoons red wine vinegar

8 tablespoons olive oil

salt and pepper

Serves 4

Spicy potato curry
with cauliflower and mustard seeds

Many Indian recipes begin with a preliminary sautéing of spices, including mustard seeds, to release their flavors and aromas. The mustard seeds will pop when they're ready. An interesting variation to this recipe, typical of Bengali cooking, is to use mustard oil instead of vegetable oil. Heating mustard oil releases wonderful warm aromas that marry well with the mild flavor of potatoes.

Heat the oil in a large skillet or wok over a medium-high heat. Add the mustard seeds and as soon as they pop, add the cumin seeds, red chiles, and bay leaves. Stir-fry for 4 to 5 seconds, then add the potatoes, cayenne pepper, turmeric, salt, and ginger. Stir to mix. Add ½ cup water. Cover and simmer for 10 minutes over a low heat. Stir in all the remaining ingredients except the tamarind paste and cook for a further 10 minutes. Stir in the tamarind. Simmer for a further 2 to 3 minutes, then remove from the heat and serve with other Indian dishes.

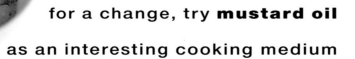

for a change, try **mustard oil**

as an interesting cooking medium

4 tablespoons
vegetable oil

½ teaspoon brown or
black mustard seeds

1 teaspoon cumin seeds

2 fresh red chiles,
seeded and chopped

2 bay leaves

1 lb. potatoes, cut
into ½-inch pieces

1½ teaspoons
cayenne pepper

½ teaspoon
ground turmeric

2 teaspoons salt

1-inch piece of fresh
gingerroot, peeled and
finely grated

2 tomatoes, chopped
into 1-inch dice

1½ tablespoons
desiccated coconut

½ tablespoon
ground coriander

2 teaspoons sugar

¾ tablespoon thick
tamarind paste

Serves 4

Accompaniments

Sweet cucumber pickle

A sweet classic pickle from Scandinavia, using European yellow mustard seeds (though you could also use black—the difference is not very great). This pickle is often served at breakfast time with a platter of cold meats such as a sweet-cured ham.

Scrub the cucumbers clean in cold water. Rinse the dill heads, if using. Peel and dice the horseradish. Place the cucumbers, dill flower heads or dill seeds, and horseradish, if using, in layers in a jar or pot. Mix all the remaining ingredients in a saucepan. Bring to a boil, skim, then pour the hot liquid over the cucumbers. Cover and chill for 3 days. Pour off the pickle liquid into a saucepan and bring it to a boil again. Pour the boiling pickle liquid over the cucumbers. Place a weight on top of the cucumbers to keep them in the pickle. Store in a dark cool place for 1 month before serving. Alternatively transfer to preserving jars for storage— the size and number of jars will depend on the size of the cucumbers.

2 lb. small green cucumbers

10 dill flower heads* or 1 tablespoon dill seeds, crushed

1 piece fresh horseradish (optional)

1¾ cups white vinegar

2¾ cups water

1¼ cups caster sugar

2 tablespoons salt

1 tablespoon yellow mustard seeds

10 white peppercorns

Makes 4 lb.

*Dill flowers are sold in some herb shops. Dill seeds are an acceptable alternative.

Green tomato pickle
with yellow mustard seeds

3 lb. green tomatoes

3 large onions

1 oz. coarse sea salt

3 cups malt vinegar

2 lb. raw sugar

1 teaspoon yellow
mustard seeds

1 teaspoon peppercorns

2 teaspoons cloves

**Makes 3 jars
of 1 pint**

Yellow mustard seeds are milder than black ones, and are often a component of European and American spice mixtures. If you grow your own tomatoes, it will be simple to pick some green ones—otherwise, you may have to order them specially from your fruit market.

Chop the tomatoes and slice the onions, then put into a pan with the remaining ingredients. Bring to a boil, then reduce to a simmer and cook slowly, stirring all the time, until the mixture is reduced to a soft pulp (about 2 hours). Pour into sterilized jars, cover, and label.

Mustard mayonnaise

2 eggs

2 tablespoons white
wine vinegar

juice of 1 lemon

2 tablespoons
mustard powder

1¼ cups mild olive oil

salt and pepper

Makes 1½ cups

Homemade mayonnaise is the best—and interestingly it is the mustard which helps the emulsification of the other ingredients.

Place the eggs, vinegar, lemon juice, mustard, salt, and pepper in a food processor or blender and process. Gradually add the oil in a thin steady stream until thickened. Serve immediately, or keep for up to 2 days in the refrigerator.

Index